Our Tremendous Lover

A devotional commentary on Solomon's Song of Songs for those who hunger for the Manifest Presence of God

Our Tremendous Lover

A devotional commentary on Solomon's Song of Songs for those who hunger for the Manifest Presence of God

Charles P. Schmitt

Printed by
Companion Press
P.O. Box 310
Shippensburg, PA 17257-0310

ISBN 1-56043-235-7

For Worldwide Distribution
Printed in the U.S.A.

This book and all other Destiny Image, Revival Press, MercyPlace, Fresh Bread, Destiny Image Fiction, and Treasure House books are available at Christian bookstores and distributors worldwide.

1 2 3 4 5 6 7 8 9 / 09 08 07 06 05 04 03

For a U.S. bookstore nearest you, call **1-800-722-6774**.
For more information on foreign distributors, call **717-532-3040**.
Or reach us on the Internet:
www.destinyimage.com

Fourth Edition, Spring 2003
Available From:
Foundational Teachings
of Immanuel's Church
16819 New Hampshire Ave.
Silver Spring, MD 20905
(301) 989-HOPE (4673)

Second Edition, Spring 1988
Third Edition, Fall 1993
Printed in the United States of America

Dedication

I dedicate this little fourteen-day devotional on Solomon's Song first of all to our beloved Lord Jesus and to His loving Bride—and in particular to those bands of bridal people presently emerging everywhere in the earth. Spiritually, the long, cold winter has passed; and the flowers of spring are appearing all across our land. This is a fresh generation of those who seek the Lord's presence!

Secondly, I dedicate this devotional to my own precious wife, Dorothy. Her love is so clearly pictured in the Shulammite's love for the shepherd; and I love her all the more, simply for that!

I also dedicate this little book to four very special young men and one very special young lady—our grandchildren: Chase Patrick, Kai Francis, Dylan Charles, Brooke Morgan and Hunter Scott. Should our heavenly Bridegroom tarry longer, I believe that all of these will grow up to become true "God Chasers," moving in the anointing of the Holy Spirit with a passion for Jesus Christ and His revival Presence, by which Jesus shall bring the nations to the feet of His heavenly Father! Amen!

Acknowledgment

I am most grateful for the careful and diligent editing of one who chooses to remain anonymous, but who will receive his open reward when Jesus, our Bridegroom, comes.

In celebration of the twentieth anniversary of Immanuel's Church

and

In celebration of Charles and Dotty's fiftieth year in ministry, and fortieth year as husband and wife

Foreword

To the Fourth Edition
A Special Anniversary Edition

The fourth edition of this little devotional commentary on the Song of Songs is also a special anniversary edition—first of all commemorating the twentieth anniversary of Immanuel's Church in Silver Spring, Maryland.

It has been amazing to me personally to trace the growth of Immanuel's Church from the fall of 1983. Beginning with a dozen people meeting in our family room, Immanuel's Church has been blesed by our Lord Jesus Christ, until at the time of this writing, Immanuel's now numbers four thousand men, women and children, many of whom are running after our Lord Jesus Christ in sincere bridal love. Thank you, Lord Jesus!

But two more anniversaries are also celebrated in the year 2003—not only the twentieth anniversary of Immanuel's Church, but the fiftieth anniversary in ministry for both my precious wife Dotty and myself; and, in turn, our own fortieth wedding anniversary!

Fifty years ago, both of us, then in our teens, having been freshly filled with the Holy Spirit, began ministering the Word of our living Lord—and we've just never stopped! Ten years later it pleased the Lord to join our lives together in marriage, for "two are better than one, because they have a good return for their labor" (Eccles. 4:9). Somehow we sense, among other things, that God's blessing on Immanuel's Church over these twenty years is part of that "good return"!

And so in this year of multiple anniversaries, we send forth this revised edition of *Our Tremendous Lover*, trusting that it will contribute to the bridal passion of the people of God upon the face of the earth, given to "hastening the coming of the day of God." Amen!

—Charles P. Schmitt
Fall, 2003

Contents

Day One

PROLOGUE: *"The Song of Songs, Which Is Solomon's"* (1:1)[1]

Of the 1,005 songs[2] composed by Solomon, king of Israel, one stands out as the song of all songs. Here is Solomon, who uses his own name seven times in this drama,[3] at his finest. This Song is the best, the most excellent of Solomon's songs because it has the most excellent theme of all—the theme of love, pure bridal love. Love is one of the major themes in the current waves of renewal and refreshing and revival that are now washing over the earth.

According to the Mishnah, Rabbi Akiba early in the second century called this Song "the holy of holies" (where the glory of God was revealed) and declared, "no day outweighed in glory the one on which Israel received the Song of Songs." It is found among the "five rolls" in the Holy Writings (the third division of the Hebrew Canon) along with Ruth, Lamentations, Ecclesiastes and Esther; and significantly enough, this Song was originally to be read on the eighth day of the Passover celebration at the beginning of the new year in Israel.

On one of our pilgrimages to Israel, while I was at the delightful Judean spring of En-gedi ("the spring of the kid") just west of the Dead Sea at the threshold of the wilderness of Judah, I felt a desire within my heart to begin this devotional commentary on the Song of Songs. Song 1:14 says, "My beloved is to me a cluster of henna blossoms in the vineyards of En-gedi"; En-gedi thus symbolizes a place of bridal love. The spring of En-gedi is bounded on the west by the barren wilderness of Judah where David fled from the jealous insanity of Saul,[4] and on the east by the deadness of the ancient Salt Sea. Yet in the midst of these two bleak areas stand the sparkling waterfalls and pools, the date trees and rich greenery of En-gedi.

The remembrance of this haunting contrast continually wooed me on to write these pages. We live in a generation in which true bridal love is surfacing in a powerful way by the Holy Spirit as He moves in fresh power across the land. The church has needed this revival of En-gedi love as it has sought to survive in the midst of this world's howling barren wilderness. We have needed to learn again how to be lovers. Now, in the midst of our fresh bridal walk with the Lord Jesus, our greatest concern must ever be a godly fear lest we lose our "first love" towards Him as did the Ephesian believers.[5]

Solomon's Song will instruct us in the themes of our love for the Lord Jesus—our tremendous Lover—and His boundless love for us, His Bride. In the Book of Ephesians, Paul introduces us to these themes using references from the Song of Songs itself: "the Beloved"[6] and "the church…having no spot."[7] I encourage you to review Ephesians 1:3-14 and 5:22-33 as a preparation for our meditation together in the Song of Songs.

The Characters of the Love Drama

For centuries, both Hebrew and Christian scholars have speculated about the identity of the main characters in this love song. Often they see but two main characters: Solomon (who appears as both king and shepherd), and the Shulammite shepherdess whose heart Solomon seeks to win. According to this view, Solomon's love for the shepherdess should not only become an encouragement to faithful and wholesome bridal love between a husband and his wife, but also as a picture of the pure love of our

Lord Jesus for His church. Though I deeply respect the authors who have written according to this understanding and accept this as a possible valid interpretation of the Song, I must confess that deep within my heart I find another interpretation to be more satisfying.

In his earliest years as king, Solomon may have qualified as an example of wholesome, faithful bridal love; yet even within this Song itself, the corrupt seeds of Solomon's well-known moral destruction are clearly evidenced. How could a man with "sixty queens and eighty concubines, and maidens without number"[8] ever become an example to us of wholesome, faithful bridal love? The king's further pursuit of still another innocent maiden to be added to his harem stands as a moral tragedy rather than an example to imitate. And how such a man, who even in his prime "loved many foreign women…from the nations concerning which the Lord had said…'you shall not associate with them…for they will surely turn your heart away after their gods' "[9]—how such a one could be a type or picture of the Lord Jesus Christ in His love for the church strains credibility.

Concerning all these women—ultimately numbering "seven hundred wives, princesses, and three hundred concubines"[10]—it is stated: "Solomon held fast to these in love."[11] And concerning them it is further recorded that "his wives turned his heart away after other gods; and his heart was not wholly devoted to the Lord his God, as the heart of David his father had been. For Solomon went after Ashtoreth the goddess of the Sidonians and after Milcom the detestable idol of the Ammonites. Solomon did what was evil in the sight of the Lord…[for] Solomon built a high place for Chemosh the detestable idol of Moab…"[12]

If anything, Solomon degenerates into a picture of spiritual corruption and backsliding, a picture of a man who has lost the very moral essence of "first love." And almost as if in support of this sober assessment, we are given the following observation in First Kings 10:14 concerning a part of Solomon's revenues from which he supported his wayward lifestyle: "Now the weight of gold which came in to Solomon in one year was *666* talents of gold," which would be about $210,000,000 in modern currency! (Please also note the reference to *666*, that same ominous number found in Revelation 13:18 so symbolic of the dark side of things.) Solomon in his fallenness is more aptly a picture of him who opposes Christ than of our Lord Jesus Christ Himself! A modern Bible commentator has stated it well when he observed: "Solomon is hardly the best example of true, loyal, single-minded love in the light of his 700 wives and 300 concubines and all the dire consequences for the nation that followed in the train of his many love affairs (see 1 Kings 11). Moreover, Solomon was no shepherd...."[13]

Solomon as a Type of Christ: The Wisdom and Glory of God

The Old Testament abounds with types and partial types of our Lord Jesus Christ. Jonah is one such partial type.[14] We would frankly have to admit that only in one aspect of his life is Jonah typical of Jesus—most certainly yes in his being "three days and three nights in the belly of the sea monster," but surely not in his stinting, ungracious, unredemptive attitude towards Nineveh.

Now the same is true with Solomon. In his glorious wisdom, Solomon *is* a picture of Christ, the vast Wisdom of God.[15] But in the very theme of this Song of Songs—that of true bridal love—Solomon in his character is a failure and most unlike our Lord Jesus. Therefore, we are impressed to look for an alternative understanding of this aspect in the little love story now before us.

An Alternative Interpretation: Three Main Characters

Solomon here writes in retrospect, as he does in Ecclesiastes, telling of his disappointing experiences in life and of the lessons he has gleaned from them. Listen wisely to the king's story. Enroute from Jerusalem, his Davidic capital in the south, to his "forest of Lebanon House"[16] in the north, Solomon passes through Shunem, a town in Issachar.[17] There, in his stopover, he falls in love with a sweet and beautiful shepherdess whom he carries off by persuasion to his courts. But much to his surprise, Solomon finds that the citadels of her heart have already been captured and held by an inconspicuous, but gracious shepherd. In the face of all of Solomon's sensual attempts to woo the woman, she nonetheless remains fiercely loyal to her one and only love, her beloved shepherd. Solomon, baffled and defeated by this turn of events, at last releases her to return to her home and her lover. In retrospect he writes this poem about a holy love that had so confused him (Song 6:5a)[18] and overwhelmed him—an awesome love that he will never forget, especially when placed alongside the promiscuous love to which he had long before sold out. In this understanding we find a real encouragement to the true and faithful bridal love of the shepherdess and her shepherd. Here we find a true picture of the virgin love between Jesus and His church.

I propose that the characters in this simple story are these: the pure and lovely shepherdess from Shunem, her shepherd-lover from Issachar, and also King Solomon; and finally, the maidens of Solomon's court ("the daughters of Jerusalem"). In the Shulammite (a by-form of Shunammite)[19] and her shepherd-lover we see both a picture of pure human bridal love and a picture of an end-time people in the throes of spiritual "first love." But in Solomon we see institutionalism, materialism, worldliness and lukewarmness. We see, according to Revelation 2–3, the decline- of that glorious early move of God at the end of the first century. The story is a warning to us who are part of this present revival move of God.

I read this Songa as a drama, so I have broken it into five movements or acts, each further divided into scenes:

Act One: Love's Restless Captivity (1:2–2:7)
Act Two: Love's Faltering Fears (2:8–3:5)
Act Three: Love's Great Conflict (3:6–5:1)
Act Four: Love's Final Choice (5:2–8:4)
Act Five: Love's Endless Triumph (8:5-14)

We will look at each scene in three segments: the Inspired Story, the biblical text; some Devotional Thoughts; and finally, Heart Searchings Before God, for our meditation and prayer.[20]

Day Two

ACT ONE: *Love's Restless Captivity*

SCENE 1: The Simple Delights of a Shepherd's Love (1:2-4a)

The Inspired Story

The Shulammite muses about her shepherd-lover (1:2a):
"Let him kiss me with the kisses of his mouth!"

Then addressing him directly, she says (1:2b–4a):
"For your loves (your caresses) are better than wine.
Your oils have a pleasing fragrance.
Your name is like precious oil poured out;
Therefore the young maidens love you!
Draw me after you," *she laughingly encourages him,*
"and let us run together!"

Devotional Thoughts

In the simplicity of this new-born rustic romance, there is nothing complicated, nothing artificial, nothing forced. Here are two lovers walking, sometimes running, together in the flowered fields of Shunem. And there the Shulammite woman's thoughts are simply—just him!

"Let *him* kiss me..." There is no need to mention his name, for there is none other. Just him! Just her beloved shepherd-lover! In her joy she declares, "All of him delights me and is precious—his kisses, his caresses, his smell, his name! Everything about him is delightful!"

Here is love in its simplicity, a first love that begs description. These qualities of gleeful delight are meant to characterize our love relationships throughout all of our life—both in the natural on the earth and also in our intimate walk with the Lord Jesus in the heavenlies.

This shepherd, just like Jesus, knew not only how to love but also how to express his love, for kisses and caresses are the springs that keep love living and dynamic.

He also knew, in his ancient context, the equivalent in our own contemporary society of using a masculine fragrance. The shepherd's "fragrant oils were sweet to smell," and it is in this same rich anointedness that Jesus comes to us in the Spirit. His fragrance fills the atmosphere, even to the point where saints have at times literally *smelled* His spicy scent! It is perhaps with this thought in mind that Paul writes of the bridal company: "We are a fragrance of Christ" (2 Cor. 2:15). As we spend time pressed close to Him we then carry His fragrance away on us.

Among his other fine qualities, the shepherd's name was quite glorious. One Hebrew translation of verse 3 states: "Like precious oil poured forth is thy name—famous afar." Likewise, the fragrance of the Name of Jesus has been spread abroad in all of its power and majesty, dignity and glory, especially in this end-time generation (see Matt. 24:14). Jesus is renowned in all the earth, drawing all men to Himself. In a recent YWAM report, Loren Cunningham wrote:

> As I constantly travel the nations of the earth, I have watched the growth of Christianity become the event of the century, while the media of the world has virtually ignored it. Look at these remarkable growth patterns: Africa in 1900, 3 percent claimed Christianity. Today over 50 percent of all Africans claim to be Christians! Latin

America in 1900, the evangelical revival began with 50,000. Today, close to 100 million claim to be dedicated followers of Christ! Today in India, 103 million claim to be Christians, with a new church born every seven minutes! In China, 1,250 are coming to Christ every hour (30,000 daily)! South Korea has 7,000 churches in Seoul alone (there were practically no churches in Korea when the century began)! In Eastern Europe, millions have come to know Christ personally since the fall of the Berlin Wall!

"Draw me after you..." are beautiful words reflecting God's boundless grace. Our whole pursuit of Jesus begins with Heaven's initiation, for "no one can come to [Jesus] unless the Father...draws him" (John 6:44). When God in His sovereignty draws us, we can then "run together" with Jesus. There is no delicate balance between law and grace; it is *all* grace. God found us when we were dead and lifeless, quickened us and raised us up and seated us together with Him in the heavenlies (see Eph. 2:5-6). *That* is grace! "Draw me after you, and let us run together!" There are always precious souls (they stand out in every place) who are literally *running* after the Lord Jesus—hungering, thirsting and pursuing Him for love's intimacies with all that is in them. Revivalist Tommy Tenny calls these "the God Chasers." The Scriptures state that these who dog His steps "wherever He goes" are "first fruits to God and to the Lamb" (Rev. 14:4), the best of the harvest! They are peculiarly *His* in His Kingdom! They have uncovered the heart of what revival and renewal and refreshing are all about!

Temple Gairdner, a missionary to the Arabs, describes his relationship with the Lord Jesus in these words: "I was walking in a world indescribably beautiful, indescribably lovely: with my heart exactly as the heart of a bride with her lover...."[21] His biographer says that "probably no friend of his who ever heard Temple Gairdner say the Name of 'Jesus' in ordinary talk can forget it...always it came out with the shy yet unconcealable note of a lover."[22] These are love's simple delights! In His Presence, sing these refreshing words, which portray the heart of every valid outpouring of God's Holy Spirit:

Loved with everlasting love,
Led by grace that love to know;
Spirit, breathing from above,
Thou hast taught me it is so.
Oh, this full and perfect peace!
Oh, this transport all divine!
In a love which cannot cease,
I am His, and He is mine.
Heav'n above is softer blue,
Earth around is sweeter green;
Something lives in ev'ry hue
Christless eyes have never seen:
Birds with gladder songs o'erflow,
Flow'rs with deeper beauties shine,
Since I know, as now I know,
I am His, and He is mine.

—G. Wade Robinson (1838-77)

Heart Searchings Before God

In my life is there need for any other, or am I fulfilled solely in Jesus? Am I pressed so close to Him that I carry away with me His fragrance? This day am I "walking in a world indescribably beautiful, indescribably lovely; with my heart exactly as the heart of a bride with her lover..."?

Lord Jesus Christ, it is simply You! Loving you is the heart of every valid move of your Holy Spirit; and this has become my heart also! You have drawn me and You continue to draw me by Your sovereign grace to run after You! This I do!

SCENE 2: THE STRANGENESS OF SOLOMON'S COURTS (1:4b-8)

The Inspired Story

The Shulammite has been carried away to Solomon's courts. (How this came about will be recounted later.) (1:4b):

"The King has brought me into his chambers," *she pines.*

In sorrowfully leaving the shepherds' fields she remembers the other gleeful maidens' words to the shepherd (1:4c):

"We will rejoice in you and be glad; we will extol your love more than wine."

Her remark to the shepherd about them was (1:4d):

"Rightly [in uprightness] do they love you."

In the inner courts of Solomon, the innocent suntanned Shulammite, quite out of character with the elegant surroundings, tremblingly confesses (1:5):

"I am very dark..."

Solomon's sympathetic concubines assure her:

"but lovely."

She confesses again to them:

"O daughters of Jerusalem, (I am) like the (dark Bedouin) tents of Kedar..."

They sympathetically counter yet again:
"Like the (*elegant white*) curtains of Solomon."
She cries out in further embarrassment (1:6):
"Do not stare at me because I am swarthy,
For the sun has burned me [has looked fiercely at me].
My mother's sons were angry with me;
They made me caretaker of the vineyards,
But I have not taken care of my own vineyard."

Then, in abject loneliness she addresses her absent shepherd (1:7):
"Tell me, O you whom my soul loves,
Where do you feed your flock,
Where do you make it rest at noon?
For why should I be like one who wanders [or, like a veiled mourner]
Beside the flocks of your companions?"

The daughters of Jerusalem sympathetically counsel her (1:8):
"If you yourself do not know,
Most beautiful among women,
Go forth on the trail of the flock,
And feed your young goats
By the tents of the shepherds (that is—*go, investigate and seek for him in the company of his fellow shepherds!*)."

Devotional Thoughts

The Shulammite has been taken to Solomon's courts. The exact story of her mishap is probably told in chapter 6:11-13. She had been wandering in the garden of nut trees, and before she was aware of it, she found herself among the encampment of the king's retinue. She started to flee, but they called after her: "Come back, come back, that we may gaze at you." They at least wanted her to do a local folk dance for them—the dance of Mahanaim, the dance of the two companies. That is how it all began. She was chosen for Solomon's pleasure.

Now she stands in the midst of his onlooking harem, very conscious of her artless naturalness. How much she is out of character with the polished elegance of Solomon's courts! The ladies of the court try to reassure her, yet she wants but one person to comfort her—her beloved shepherd. "Tell me, O you whom my soul loves, where do you feed your flock, where do you make it rest at noon?"

Throughout this act, the Shulammite maiden impersonally refers to Solomon as "the king" (1:4,12); but of her shepherd-lover she speaks in the most endearing terms: "O you whom my soul loves"; and "my beloved." Solomon has carried her away to his lavish courts in one grand attempt to overwhelm her and win her heart, but he does not realize how bonded her heart is to that simple, obscure shepherd of Issachar.

The Shulammite is the symbol of simplicity and purity; she is what the revived, renewed, refreshed Bride of Christ is to be in the midst of this fallen, materialistic and gaudy world. We are presently in the midst of a powerful and widespread visitation of the manifest Presence of God from the heavens. The Spirit of God has broken forth as sun and wind and rain upon the earth, and there is an apostolic simplicity and purity, a restoration of bridal love that is emerging everywhere. But, as in the first century, insidious forces are at work,; mischievous little foxes are already creeping in, seeking to spoil the vines. Solomon, the "fallen" man, is seeking his entrance. He wants to steal away the heart of the Bride, to win her away from her Lover.

Cares Versus Love

In verse 6 of this little scene, the shepherdess speaks of her *doings*—"*caretaker* of the vineyards," and of her failings—"I have *not taken care* of my own vineyard." But in her ensuing cry she lifts her thoughts from her cares and centers them on loving: "O you whom my soul loves." True, we are called to be *laborers* but first we must be lovers. Only out of our abounding loving relationship with Jesus is strength born to win the nations to the feet of our God. Amy Carmichael, twentieth-century missionary to south India, who experienced both a powerful revival as well as a vast harvest of souls, caught the vision for such communion in her words:

> *Walking the dawn-wind, with Jesus, Heavenly Lover.*
> *In the still beauty of the waking morn, unveil Thyself to me,*
> *And with that vision shall come the strength for trials yet unborn.*

Concerning the revival at Dohnavur, Miss Carmichael wrote:

> It was so startling and dreadful—I can use no other word...Soon the whole upper half of the church was on its face on the floor crying to God...The sound was like the sound of strong wind in the trees...the hurricane of prayer continued for over four hours...almost the whole compound got saved....[23]

Charles Wesley (1707-88), who lived and labored in the great, far-spread eighteenth-century Methodist revival, wrote a hymn based on the very verses we are pondering in Solomon's Song:

Thou Shepherd of Israel, and mine,
The joy and desire of my heart,
For closer communion I pine,
I long to reside where Thou art.

The pasture I languish to find,
Where all who their Shepherd obey,
Are fed on His bosom reclined,
And screened from the heat of the day.

'Tis there, with the lambs of Thy flock,
There only I covet to rest;
To lie at the foot of the Rock,
Or rise to be hid in Thy breast.

'Tis there I would always abide,
And never a moment depart,
Concealed in the cleft of Thy side,
Eternally hid in Thy heart.

Heart Searchings Before God

Am I full of cares—even cares for His work, cares that distract my heart from loving Jesus? Or am I one given to "walking the dawn-wind with Jesus, Heavenly Lover"?

Lord Jesus, You have called me initially not to care, but to love. I turn away from all those cares—even the cares of Your kingdom—that would choke the simplicity of my virgin love for You. In "the still beauty of the waking morn," I seek You, Lord Jesus. And I cleave to my love-relationship with You, knowing that birthed out of it shall come the strength for labors in Your vineyard. Amen.

Day Four

SCENE 3: The Scene at Solomon's Table
(1:9-14)

The Inspired Story

Reclining at his banquet table, Solomon flatters the beautiful Shulammite (1:9-10):

"I compare you, my darling, to my mare among the chariots of Pharaoh" (*a lofty compliment in Eastern culture*).

"Your cheeks are beautiful with ornaments, your neck with strings of beads" (she had been bedecked and bejeweled for the occasion by the attendants of the harem).

These attendants add (1:11):

"We will make for you ornamental chains of gold studded with silver."

Objectively mentioning King Solomon in passing, the Shulammite then subjectively speaks of her absent shepherd-lover (1:12-14):

"While the king reclined at his table, my spikenard perfume ('*my absent lover*'[24]) gave forth its fragrance.

"My beloved (*shepherd*) is to me a sachet of myrrh which lies all night between my breasts. (*According to the Mishnah, Hebrew women were accustomed to wearing little pouches of myrrh, hanging them from their necks between their breasts.*)

"My beloved (*shepherd*) is to me a cluster of henna blossoms from the vineyards of En-gedi (*renowned for its vineyards and its aromatic shrubs*)."

Devotional Thoughts

The scene is in Solomon's palace at his lavish banqueting table. From Solomon's flattery and the enthusiasm of the surrounding attendants, it would seem the Shulammite has everything going for her; nonetheless, she is quite lonely. She can think only of her beloved shepherd. He is the sweetness of her life, and nothing but him can satisfy her.

The late John Deane from New Zealand, in his little devotional booklet entitled, *This Tremendous Lover* (from which I had derived so many of my own insights), observed:

> King Solomon had swept this lovely country lass off to his palace, and thought to win her affection; but his palace and person and promises and praise meant nothing to her. To all his words her reply was instant, as she thought of the lad she loved: "My Love is to me a bundle of myrrh...My Love is to me a cluster of henna flowers..." Her absent Lover's love was the very perfume of her life.... How truly and completely her heart had been won by that pure-hearted country lover. He had filled her soul with his love, and she could not but be true to him.[25]

In our generation the world is especially filled with broken hearts, with shattered loves, with severed marriages. Somehow the sons of men have not captured the pureness of the fidelity of this shepherdess to her shepherd-lover. The Song of Songs, by comparison, is a refreshing story of fierce loyalty. There was frankly no room in the Shulammite's heart for Solomon to attract her. She was *totally* satisfied with her beloved and *completely* taken up with him. And the same was true of him towards her. May I suggest that we lay our hearts open before the Lord Jesus Christ for Him to search us out. Do we know what it is to be faithful, to be loyal, to be steadfast, to be committed in our covenant relationships? Only the cleansing mercies and the empowering grace of Jesus can make us so!

Solomon: The Waning Glory of the Church

In many ways the story of the church is like the story of King Solomon. What began on the Day of Pentecost as a powerfully anointed expression of God's wisdom and glory, out of which the magnificent dwelling place of God, the Church, would be built, soon dwindled in might and effectiveness. Arthritic with age and declining in strength, the fading apostolic church soon corrupted itself in spiritual adultery and spiritual idolatry (just as Solomon, who had such a good beginning, eventually did). This sin, notwithstanding ongoing moves of revival in virtually every century, inevitably brought division. In Solomon's history it was the painful division between north and south, between Judah and Israel. In the history of the church it was the divisions between East and West in the eleventh century, between the Roman Church and the Reformers in the sixteenth century, and multiplied divisions among Christians ever since.

But currently we are experiencing days of marvelous renewal, refreshing, revival, and restoration that are overflowing into every segment of a previously fragmented Christianity and creating a new unity in the Body of Christ. Pastors from different denominations are beginning to pray together, seeking God's face for revival. Churches are beginning to come together for worship and intercession, pursuing the Lord together for His purposes. In the Washington, D.C. area we are presently seeing marvelous happenings along these lines, as we are collectively seeking God to pour out His Spirit on our nation's capital. This is indeed a day of "new beginnings"! As a result a bridal company is being prepared on earth, with its matching counterpart in the heavenlies, that will be presented to Jesus our heavenly Lover at His return—a Bride "in all her glory, having no spot or wrinkle [having neither adolescent blemishes nor old-age wrinkles, literally] or any such thing; but…holy and blameless"! (Eph. 5:27)

God is indeed raising up a people—a holy, bridal people—who will determinedly defy every subtle snare of the enemy and passionately press on into "hastening the coming of the day of God"! (2 Pet. 3:12)

Bernard of Clairvaux (1090-1153), himself a medieval revivalist and a rare bridal soul, expressed these thoughts in the words of a hymn:

Jesus, the very thought of Thee
With sweetness fills my breast;
But sweeter far Thy face to see,
And in Thy presence rest.

Jesus, our only joy be Thou,
As Thou our Prize wilt be;
Jesus, be Thou our Glory now,
And through eternity.

Heart Searchings Before God

Do I "have eyes for no one but Jesus"? Is Jesus "the very perfume of my life"? Is anything else, anyone else, my ultimate joy and prize and glory?

Lord Jesus Christ, on every hand the glitter of Solomon's courts would attract me: the lustings of the flesh, the desires of the eyes, the boastful vanities of this life. Fix my heart, Lord Jesus, until it is wholly set upon You, wholly abandoned to You! Keep my heart pure within me—pure for You!

Day Five

Scene 4: The Sweetness of the Shulammite's Recollections (1:15–2:7)

The Inspired Story

The scene now shifts to another part of the king's palace. In recalling the sweet words of her shepherd-lover and of her own tender responses to him, the Shulammite is encouraged (1:15):

"Behold, how beautiful you are, my darling," he had declared.
Behold, how beautiful you are!
Your eyes are doves."

And she responded to him (1:16-17):

"Behold, how handsome you are, my beloved, and so pleasant!

Indeed our couch is leafy green (*luxuriant*). The beams of our (*simple*) house—*in contrast to this awesome palace*—are cedars; our rafters, cypresses."

Thus emboldened, she firmly addresses Solomon who has just entered (2:1):

"I am (*only*) a crocus of the plain of Sharon, a (*little*) lily of the valleys. (*You are mistaken in thinking me adaptable to these artificial surroundings, imposing as they are.*[26])"

Solomon quickly interjects (2:2):

"Like a lily among the thorns,
So is my darling among the daughters (by comparison)."

But she can only speak of her past experiences with her absent lover (2:3-6):

"As an apple tree among the trees of the forest,
So is my beloved among the sons.
In his shade I took great delight and sat down,
And his fruit was sweet to my palate.
He brought me to the house of wine (the banqueting house)
And his banner over me was love."

"Sustain me with raisin cakes, refresh me with apples,"
she cries,

"For I am lovesick" (*expressing the intense longing of one separated from her beloved*).

"O that his left hand were under my head, and his right hand were embracing me!"

Sensing the futility of further effort, at least for the time being, Solomon admonishes the ladies of the court (2:7):

"I charge you, O daughters of Jerusalem,

By the gazelles or by the hinds of the field (*which are free to follow their own instincts*[27])

That you will not arouse or awaken my love[28] until she pleases." (*The other acts close in this fashion as well*—3:5; [cf. also 5:8]; 8:4.)

Devotional Thoughts

The Shulammite maiden stands alone in Solomon's palaces. She now draws strength from her recollections of sweet communion with her beloved in days past. To him, she was beautiful with "dove's eyes";—to her, he was "handsome" and "so pleasant." She prefers all that he is and all that his house is, to all of Solomon and his house.

In the Hebrew the meaning is clear: not that her eyes are *like* doves' eyes but her eyes *are* doves! Doves have the amazing ability to focus singly on but one object at a time. This singleness of the Shulammite's vision had captured the shepherd's heart (and will frustrate Solomon). A beautiful translation of Hebrews 12:2a reads as follows: "having eyes for no one but Jesus"; this sums up what doves' eyes are all about.

Doves are also utterly faithful and loyal. Someone told me that once a pair has mated, they are mated for life. Should one die, the remaining mate will often just pine away. At our Maryland home, which backs up to parklands, a pair of mourning doves visits daily the little bird sanctuary we have created. The evidence of their loyalty and their faithfulness to each other is an inspiration! In this generation of covenant-breaking, husbands and wives continually need to produce sounds of loyalty and notes of constancy: "Your eyes are doves: you are committed and faithful, loyal and true!"

In contrast to all that Solomon is, this obscure shepherd boy appears so ruggedly "handsome...beloved, and so pleasant" (1:16). In contrast to all that Solomon's imperial palaces offer, the artlessness of the shepherd's house is what the bride is committed to—"our couch is leafy green...The beams of our house are cedars; our rafters, cypresses" (1:17). It is not even that the beams of this house are *made of* cedars; they are cedars, growing cedars. The rafters are not merely *made of* cypresses; they are cypresses, living cypresses. Likewise, the Lord's church is a living house. It is His habitation—the ongoing dwelling of His Presence with us! (see Eph. 2:21) By worldly standards, Solomon's prestigious palace of today, with all its silver and gold and quarried stone and silken tapestries, *should* evidence the presence and power of God. To the contrary, the halls of Solomon's institutional sanctuaries are all too often dead and deadening! But a fresh thing is emerging in the earth, and David's tabernacle is being rebuilt (see Acts 15:16). Its one characteristic is *life*: unaffected, anointed, spontaneous, apostolic life! In the midst of all that Solomon has to offer, the Bride, as a humble crocus of Sharon's plain (2:1), is totally misfitted. She has been built for better things!

In the Secret of His Presence

The Shulammite describes her memories of sweet communion with her beloved shepherd. He stands out in singular fashion "as an apple tree among the trees of the forest." She speaks of sheltering herself in his shadow and satisfying herself in his sweetness: "In his shade I took great delight and sat down, and his fruit was sweet to my palate." John Deane speaks of having "a trysting place," a secret place for daily sweet communion with the Lord Jesus.

Ellen L. Goreh, a hymnwriter, lived in the mid-to-late nineteenth century, in a time of unusual worldwide revival. In the United States, out of a population of 30 million, one million people were converted to Christ in one year! Likewise, all across the United Kingdom, a million people found the Lord! One eyewitness writes: "Such a time as the present was never known since the days of the Apostles...Revivals now cover our land, sweeping all before them, exciting the earnest cry from thousands, 'what shall we do to be saved?'...It really seems as if the Millennium was upon us in its glory."[29]

Just listen to these words in Ellen Goreh's "trysting place" hymn; they contain the secret to revival:

In the secret of His presence how my soul delights to hide!
Oh, how precious are the lessons which I learned at Jesus' side!

Earthly cares can never vex me, neither trials lay me low;
For when Satan comes to tempt me, to the secret place I go.
When my soul is faint and thirsty, 'neath the shadow of His wing
There is cool and pleasant shelter, and a fresh and crystal spring;
And my Saviour rests beside me, as we hold communion sweet;
If I tried, I could not utter what He says when thus we meet.

Would you like to know the sweetness of the secret of the Lord?
Go and hide, beneath His shadow; this shall then be your reward,
And when'er you leave the silence of that happy meeting-place,
You will bear the shining image of the Master in your face.

Do you have such a daily secret "trysting place" for meeting with the Lord Jesus?

This first act in the Song of Solomon ends with two stirring pleas. The Shulammite, lovesick for her absent shepherd, cries out for his embraces (2:5-6). And Solomon, sensing the futility of presently wooing her any further, admonishes the ladies of his harem to leave the Shulammite alone—hoping that somehow, someday, she will spontaneously love him (2:7). Unfortunately for Solomon, that will never be. The Shulammite's heart has already been sealed to another!

Heart Searchings Before God

Do I have a "dove's eyes"? Am I utterly faithful and loyal in my covenant relationships, and in my walk with Jesus, my heavenly Lover? Do I have a quiet place and a quiet hour for my Beloved? Do I have, and cherish having, a secret place for meeting with the Son of God? Revivals are birthed in just such an atmosphere of seeking Him with passionate and strong desire; and they are only maintained in that same holy environment!

Lord Jesus, I would have eyes, a dove's eyes, for no one but You! And I do seek You—early and late—to know the secret of Your presence! By Your grace make me loyal in my walk in the heavenlies and in my walk upon the earth as I press into Your holy presence!

Day Six

ACT TWO: *Love's Faltering Fears*

SCENE 1: The Suddenness of the Shepherd's Appearing (2:8-17)

The Inspired Story

The scene is early springtime.. Solomon and his retinue have returned to his Jerusalem palace, bringing the Shulammite with them. An unexpected visitor now comes to the palace walls.

The shepherdess excitedly informs the ladies of the court (2:8-9):

"Listen! My beloved!
Behold—this very one—he is coming!
Leaping upon the mountains,
Bounding (skipping) over the hills!
My beloved is like a gazelle or a young stag.
Behold—this very one—he is standing behind our wall,
He is looking through the windows,
He is peering (blooming) through the lattice!"

She later recounts the shepherd's words to her, he having pled with her to leave Solomon's courts (2:10-14):

"My beloved responded and said to me,
'Arise, my darling, my beautiful one,
And come along—come away with me!
For behold, the winter is past,[30]
The rain is over and gone.

The flowers have already appeared in the land;
The time has arrived for singing (pruning),
And the voice of the turtledove has been heard in our land.
The fig tree has ripened its (winter) figs,
And the vines in blossom have given forth their fragrance.
Arise, my darling, my beautiful one,
And come along—come away with me!

'O, my dove, in the clefts of the crag (*for so Solomon's fortress-like palace appeared to him*),
In the secret place of the steep cliffs,[31]
Let me see your appearance,
Let me hear your voice;
For your voice is sweet,
And your appearance is lovely.' "

And then he soberly enjoins (2:15):
"Catch for us the foxes, the young foxes
That are ruining the vineyards (by burrowing),
For our vineyards are in blossom."

To the excited ladies of the court who surround her, she remarks (2:16):
"My beloved is mine, and I am his;
He is feeding (his flock) among the lilies (*of the fields*)."[32]

But to the shepherd (perhaps out of fear for his safety, should he be found near the harem) she speaks these "goodbye" words (2:17):
"Until the day cool (*with evening breezes*) and the shadows flee away,

Turn, my beloved, and be like a gazelle
Or a young stag on the mountains of separation."[33]

Devotional Thoughts

Excitedly, the shepherdess alerts the maidens of the harem to the appearance of her beloved. He has come in this beautiful springtime from Issachar to Jerusalem to bid her come away with him. Her appearance and her voice are a delight to him and he can only treasure her as his very own. He would have her go forth with him to their native fields and meadows: "Arise, my darling, my beautiful one, and come along—come away with me!" But out of fear she sends him away.

The sheer excitement of this humble maiden at the appearance of her beloved shepherd (2:8-9) can be only a reflection of how a bridal people are to "*love* his appearing" (see 2 Tim. 4:8 AV). The second coming of our Lord Jesus Christ was never intended to be a sterile dogma over which the church would wrangle and divide, but was meant to be a *rapturous* happening: the meeting of two lovers, a bride and a groom (hence the term "rapture"). The restoration of bridal love (see Acts 3:20-21) will most certainly draw Jesus from the heavens, for Jesus "will appear a second time…*to those who eagerly await Him*" (Heb. 9:28). Is your heart so *eagerly awaiting Him*? Do you so love His appearing? If so, in this, you are hastening the coming of the day of the Lord.

It is springtime in our story. One translation of the words "your first love" in Revelation 2:4 reads this way: "the springtime of your love." The Ephesian believers had lost that. And it is not difficult to do. Even in outpourings of the Holy Spirit and in our service to God, it is possible to lose that springtime of our love for the Lord Jesus. John Deane has described springtime as follows:

> Winter's wind and frost have gone. The land has clothed herself in bridal array. The warm air and the sun's caresses have called to sleeping seed and flower...The gentle turtledove nestles near its mate...The fragrance of the bursting buds fills the air; and the shepherd-lover calls to his lassie to go forth with him. Springtime has come.[34]

Oh, to live in that season of refreshing, to breathe that air, to enjoy that revival atmosphere—that awesome Presence of God—perpetually! Oh, to be forever *in love*! Such is the hallmark of every godly marriage; and such is the essence of our bridal union with Jesus. Unfortunately, though, this is the easiest thing to lose! It is the *heart* of all renewal; it is the *heart* of every valid revival move of God; yet usually it is the *first* element to depart! Spirit of the Living God, help us! Help us in our homes; and help us continue on "in love" (a phrase Paul so beautifully uses five times in the letter to the Ephesians: 1:4; 4:2; 4:15-16; 5:2).

The shepherd's words in Song 2:14b are impressive: "Let me see your appearance, let me hear your voice; for your voice is sweet, and your appearance is lovely." These words reflects Jesus' great delight in us, His Bride. To Him *our* voice is sweet; to Him *our* appearance is lovely. We are His treasure; we are His rich inheritance. Perhaps, and rightly so, our emphasis has for so long been on how rich *we* are in Him and on how great an inheritance *we* have in Him. But in Ephesians 1:18 Paul prays that an inward illumination may come to the church so that we might know "what are the riches of the glory of *His* inheritance in the saints"—that is to say, how rich *He* is in us and how great an inheritance *He* has in having us! How great is *His* delight in you, in me, this very day! Perhaps now we can begin to understand something of exactly why "he lavished upon us…the riches of His grace" (Eph. 1:8, 7). He did so because He so deeply and tenderly and faithfully loves us! We are His treasure, His delight!

He repeatedly calls us to abandonment, utter abandonment to Himself: "Arise, my darling, my beautiful one, and come away with me!" (2:10, 13) His deep concern is for utter consecration and an awe-inspiring holiness—"Catch for us the foxes, those little foxes that are ruining the vineyards" (2:15). Only in the strength of knowing how much we mean to Him can we rise up and run after Him. Only then can we purge our vineyards of those gnawing, yipping young foxes (what the New Testament writer terms "every encumbrance, and the sin which so easily entangles us") so that we might "run with endurance the race that is set before us, [having eyes for no one but Jesus]!" (Heb. 12:1-2a)

"My beloved is mine, and I am his" (2:16a). No more all-encompassing confession could ever be uttered by the saint of God.

Oh, I am my Beloved's,
And my Beloved's mine!
He brings a poor vile sinner
Into His "House of Wine,"
I stand upon His merit,
I know no other stand,
Not e'en where glory dwelleth
In Immanuel's land.

O Christ, He is the fountain,
he deep, sweet well of love,
The streams on earth I've tasted,
More deep I'll drink above,
There to an ocean fullness

His mercy doth expand,
And glory, glory dwelleth
In Immanuel's land.
—Anne R. Cousin (1824-1906)

Heart Searchings Before God

Am I "in love" with Jesus? Am I eagerly waiting for Him from heaven? Am I loving His soon appearing? Do I see how rich a treasure I am to Him; how greatly He loves me and how much He desires me? In the strength of that revelation, have I purged my vineyard of those yipping, nipping young foxes—those subtle compromises—which would ultimately spoil the tender vines from producing godly fruit?

Lord Jesus Christ, our tremendous Lover, I hear Your voice and I rise up, in springtime abandon, to run after You with all that is within me!

Day Seven

Scene 2: The Sorrowfulness of the Shepherd's Absence (3:1-5)

The Inspired Story

Having bidden her beloved to depart (2:17), *the Shulammite now recounts her dreams in which she searches for him* (3:1):

"On my bed night after night[35] I sought him
Whom my soul loves;
I sought him but did not find him."

And she announces (3:2a):

"I will arise now and go about the city;
In the streets and in the broad ways
I will seek him whom my soul loves."

But her search proved initially fruitless (3:2b-3):

"I sought him but did not find him.
The watchmen who make the rounds in the city found me (to whom I asked),
'Have you seen him whom my soul loves?'"

But then, as she dreamed further (3:4):

"Scarcely had I left them
When I found him whom my soul loves;
I held on to him and would not let him go,
Until I had brought him to my mother's house,
And into the chamber of her who conceived me."

Upon hearing the account of this dream, Solomon, again sensing the futility of further trying to persuade the Shulammite to desire him, admonishes the ladies of his court (3:5):

"I charge you, O daughters of Jerusalem,

By the gazelles or by the hinds of the field (which are free to follow their own instincts[36])

That you will not arouse or awaken my love,[37]

Until she pleases."

Devotional Thoughts

The previous scene closed with the young country girl sending her beloved away, probably for his safety. Consequently, she is tossing night after night on her bed, dreaming of pursuing him.

At this point may I offer a personal conviction? Peter reminds us in his second epistle that the coming of our Lord Jesus Christ does not hinge solely on an act of God's sovereign will. There is to be a people upon the earth—a passionate, prophetic, pure people—who will be found "*hastening* the coming of the day of God" (2 Pet. 3:12). Well may we then ask, Why has the coming of the day of God apparently been delayed these past several thousand years? The answer could be, in part, that the people of God have not hastened it along but have hindered it instead.

I personally believe it had been the Lord's desire to have returned for His Bride even within the first century. Had not Peter declared in his own day: "The end of all things *has come new*" (1 Pet. 4:7 mg.)? Had not John heard Jesus say, "Behold, I am coming *quickly*" (Rev. 22:12)? I sense that as the church moved from simplicity to structure, from passion to passivity, the Bride of Christ on the earth—already entangled in "the affairs of Solomon"—actually thereby turned her Beloved away. And the history of the church from that hour until now, especially through these last centuries of reformation and restoration, renewal, and revival, has been one of tossing and turning throughout this entire dark night, in pursuit of her Beloved One. And perhaps, beyond all else which is being restored to the church today, this one passion is now the most important—a desire for His return! A.B. Simpson, had it, for he would often speak of "bringing back the King." That same desire is catching fresh fire today in the hearts of a bridal people across the face of the earth: a passion to finish the task of worldwide harvest and thereby hasten the coming of the day of the Lord! This is the finale of all that God is after—the personal return of our Lord Jesus for His beloved people, His glorious Bride, and the return of our obscure and lowly Shepherd as the reigning, triumphant, glorious King of all kings and Lord of all lords. I can think of nothing grander to give my whole life for! Can you?

The Pursuit of God

Separation between lovers is painful, especially when the separation has its roots in unbelief and fear. Night after night in her dreams, and day after day in her waking hours, the Shulammite is in pursuit of her absent shepherd-lover. The verbs themselves in this passage are a study in the art of pursuit. "I *sought* him…I *sought* him…I will *seek* him…I *sought* him…" Four times in this passage the maiden crowns him with the loving expression, "him whom my soul loves." And her dreams end in the joyous expressions: "I found him…I held on to him…I brought him…"

Some years ago, a religious slogan, "I found *it*," actually summarized our greatest evangelical weakness. Many people pursue an "it"—an experience of salvation, a blessing, a work of grace, something *from* God. But currently bridal souls pursue *Him*—the

Lord Jesus Himself. They passionately seek His *face* and not just His *hand* (see 2 Chron. 7:14). Not merely what He can *do* for us, but who He *is*. Not just salvation, but the Savior. Not merely gifts, but the Giver. Not only sanctification, but the Holy One Himself. Not simply the Body of Christ, but Christ Himself the Head of the Body. "I sought *Him*...I found *Him*..."

A.W. Tozer clearly addresses this matter in his challenging book, *The Pursuit of God*:

> To have found God and still to pursue Him is the soul's paradox of love, scorned indeed by the too-easily-satisfied religionist, but justified in happy experience by the children of the burning heart. St. Bernard [of Clairvaux, 1090–1153] stated this holy paradox in a musical quatrain that will be instantly understood by every worshipping soul:
>
> We taste Thee, O thou Living Bread,
> And long to feast upon Thee still.
> We drink of Thee, the Fountainhead,
> And thirst our souls from Thee to fill.
>
> Come near to the holy men and women of the past and you will soon feel the heat of their desire after God. They mourned for Him, they prayed and wrestled and sought for Him day and night, in season and out, and when they had found Him the finding was all the sweeter for the long seeking.[38]

The open return of our glorious Shepherd-Lover in all of His splendor and majesty will be the finale to this inner holy pursuit of men and women after God. To those who have sought Him that He might dawn and arise *in their hearts* (see 2 Pet. 1:19), He will then be revealed from heaven in flaming splendor "when He comes to be glorified in His saints on that day, and to be marveled at among all who have believed" (2 Thess. 1:10). Listen!

> *There's a light upon the mountains, and the day is at the spring,*
> *When our eyes shall see the beauty and the glory of the King ...*
>
> *In the fading of the starlight we can see the coming morn;*
> *And the lights of men are paling in the splendors of the dawn ...*
>
> *There's a hush of expectation, and a quiet in the air:*
> *And the breath of God is moving in the fervent breath of prayer ...*
>
> *Hark! we hear a distant music, and it comes with fuller swell,*
> *'Tis the triumph-song of Jesus, of our King, Immanuel ...*
>
> —Henry Burton (1840–1930)

Heart Searchings Before God

Am I in pursuit of the Lord Jesus *Himself*? Do I seek His Face (who He is) and not merely His Hand (what He can do for me)? Do I prize *Him* and His presence above all His graces and gifts and good things? Have I found my satisfaction in the presence of the Lord Jesus, or am I still drawing my joys from the *things* of the Lord? Am I part of that holy bridal company upon the earth that is longingly drawing the Lord Jesus from heaven?

Lord Jesus, I desire to desire You preeminently. I take You, this day, as the great Lover of my soul. To have You is sufficient to all my need! I seek Your Face!

And—maranatha! O, my Lord, come! Hurry, my Beloved. Come quickly, O Lord Jesus! Come!

Day Eight

ACT THREE: *Love's Great Conflict*

SCENE 1: The Show and Pomp of Solomon

(3:6–4:6)

The Inspired Story

Solomon is again enroute from Jerusalem to the northern summer palace. A group of onlookers cries out in amazement at the dazzling sight of his entourage (3:6):

"Who is this coming up from the wilderness
Like pillars of smoke (*possibly, clouds of dust caused by the procession*),
Perfumed with myrrh and frankincense,
From all kinds of fragrant powders of the merchant?"

One of the more knowledgeable onlookers answers (3:7-8):

"Behold, it is the traveling couch of Solomon;
Sixty mighty men around it,
Of Israel's mighty men.
All of them are wielders of the sword,
Expertly instructed in war.
Each man is holding his sword,
Watching against the terror of the nights."

Another, somewhat more informed, adds this description (3:9-10):

"King Solomon has made for himself a carrying chair (palanquin)
From the trees of Lebanon.

He made its poles of silver,
Its back of gold,
And its riding seat of purple,
With its interior lined with love
By the daughters of Jerusalem."

Then, the courier's solemn cry goes up (3:11):
"Go forth, O daughters of Zion,
And look on King Solomon with the crown
With which his mother (Bathsheba) had crowned him
On the day of his wedding,
And on the day of the gladness of his heart."[39]

Solomon then addresses the Shulammite girl in eloquent oratory (4:1-5):
"Behold, you are beautiful, my darling,
Behold, you are beautiful!
Your eyes are doves behind your veil (*he, too, recognized her singleness of vision*).
Your hair is like a flock of goats
Which trail down Mount Gilead.
Your teeth are like a flock of evenly shorn ewes
Which have come up from their washing place,
All of which bear twins,
And not one among them is barren.
Your lips are like a thread of scarlet,
And your mouth is lovely.
Your temples are like a slice of pomegranate
Behind your veil.[40]
Your neck is like the tower of David
Built for an arsenal,

On which hang a thousand shields,
All the shields of the mighty men.
Your two breasts are like two fawns,
Twins of a gazelle,
Which feed among the lilies."

At this last, most intimate reference, the embarrassed Shulammite can only excuse herself from Solomon's presence (4:6):

"Until the day cool off and the shadows flee away,
I will go myself to the mountain of myrrh
And to the hill of frankincense."

Devotional Thoughts

In his splendor, Solomon is impressive and singular, surrounded by his royal guard, carried on his royal palanquin. He fills all the vision of the daughters of Jerusalem—"Go forth, O daughters of Zion, and look on King Solomon..." But one alone remains unimpressed, the very one Solomon most desires to captivate. To him, she is stunningly beautiful to behold—her eyes, her hair, her teeth, her mouth, her lips, her temples, her neck. But all of his flattery is to no avail She is her beloved's and his alone. In solitude, the Shulammite leaves Solomon's presence to walk alone in the mountain evening.

Solomon is characterized by notoriety and calls attention to himself by garish splendor and gilded splash (Song 3:6-11): "Behold, King Solomon..." (cf. Song 3:7,11). In contrast, the shepherd is hidden and unknown, so much so that the ladies of the court finally ask the maiden, *Who exactly is this one you are so in love with, and where is he to be found?* (cf. 5:9; 6:1). Were

Solomon the Shulammite's true lover, the ladies of the court would not have to inquire. Between these two characteristics—obscurity and notoriety—lies the difference between the fresh move of God and the sterile religious movements of the day. The move of God often remains unobtrusive, unknown, unheralded. But in its obscurity and modesty, the grass roots movement of God's Spirit is infiltrating everything everywhere in this present generation; and out of it a virgin Bride is emerging. Veiled from Solomon, she is betrothed to one Husband. Simplicity and purity are her twin characteristics (see 2 Cor. 11:2-3), the very characteristics of her Shepherd-Lover Himself.

Empty Eloquencies

Do you ever wonder how many times Solomon had already uttered the eloquencies of Song 4:1-5 over many other women? As he touches certain intimacies about the shepherdess, she blushingly excuses herself from his presence to walk pensively alone in the cool of the evening. Her thoughts and her conclusions could perhaps best be summed up in the song of Jane C. Bonar:

Fade, fade, each earthly joy;
Jesus is mine!
Break every tender tie;
Jesus is mine.
Dark is the wilderness;
Earth has no resting place;
Jesus alone can bless;
Jesus is mine!
Tempt not my soul away;
Jesus is mine!
Here would I ever stay;
Jesus is mine.

Perishing things of clay,
Born but for one brief day,
Pass from my heart away;
Jesus is mine!
Farewell, ye dreams of night;
Jesus is mine!
Lost in this dawning bright,
Jesus is mine.
All that my soul has tried
Left but a dismal void;
Jesus has satisfied;
Jesus is mine!

Heart Searchings Before God

Is my heart virgin in simplicity and purity before Jesus? Am I free from Solomon's gilded courts? Or does this fleshly world with all its sterile religious systems cloud my view of Jesus?

Lord Jesus Christ, You have sealed my heart for Yourself. Here would I ever stay! Jesus, You are mine! Let everything else fade from my sight, leaving You alone! I love You, my dear Lord Jesus, with all my heart!

Day Nine

SCENE 2: THE SINCERITY AND PLEADINGS OF THE SHEPHERD (4:7–5:1)

The Inspired Story

As the Shulammite thoughtfully walks alone in the cool of the mountain evening, one has been quietly following her, watching her from the bushes. Suddenly the shepherd steps forth and speaks (4:7):

"You are altogether beautiful, my darling,
And there is no blemish—no flaw, no spot—in you."[41]

He then pleads with her to flee the Lebanon summer home of Solomon and return with him to the fields of Shunem (4:8):

"Come with me from Lebanon, my bride,
Come with me from Lebanon.
Journey (leap) down from the summit of Amana,
From the summit of Senir and Hermon,[42]
From the dens of lions (*for so he viewed Solomon's palace*),
From the mountains of leopards."

Then, in a most refreshing expression of tender joy, the shepherd cries out (4:9-11):

"You have made my heart beat faster (you have ravished my heart), my sister, my bride:

You have made my heart beat faster (you have ravished my heart) with a single (glance) of your eyes,

With a single strand of your necklace.

How beautiful are your loves, my sister, my bride!
How much better are your loves than wine,
And the fragrance of your perfumes
Than all kinds of spices!
Your lips, my bride, drip honey;
Honey and milk are under your tongue,
And the fragrance of your outer garments is like the fragrance of Lebanon."

He praises her for her resistance to Solomon's allurements; she is sealed and locked shut to all others but to him! (4:12-15):
"A garden locked (bolted) is my sister, my bride,
A rock garden (a spring) locked, a fountain sealed up.
(*For me alone*) your shoots (plants) are a paradise of pomegranates
With choicest fruits, henna with spikenard,
Spikenard and saffron, calamus cane and cinnamon,
With all trees of frankincense,
Myrrh and aloes, along with all the finest balsam spices.
(*For me alone you are*) a garden spring (a fountain of gardens),
A well of living waters,
And flowing (rushing) streams from Lebanon."

In response, she can only open up herself all the more to him whom her soul so loves (4:16):
"Awaken, 0 North Wind (*with deeper dealings*)
And come, Wind of the South (*with tender comforts*).
Make my garden breathe forth fragrance,
Let its spices flow out.

Let my beloved come into his garden (*her heart and her love had been locked to all others but to him*)

And eat his choicest fruits!"

He responds joyfully (5:1):

"I have come into my garden, my sister, my bride;

I have gathered my myrrh along with my spice,

I have eaten my honeycomb with my honey;

I have drunk my wine with my milk."

Then addressing his companions of the fields, he invites them to be likewise blessed by her love:

"Eat, O friends;

Drink and drink fully, O beloved ones."

Devotional Thoughts

The shepherd fervently pleads with the Shulammite to leave Lebanon and return with him to Shunem. He delights in her, for she has ravished his heart by merely one of her glances. She has remained loyal to him—closed to Solomon's advances, but very open to him. And she wants him to have full access to her life: "Let my beloved come into his garden...."

Despite all of King Solomon's eloquent words to the Shulammite maiden, the shepherd alone has the right to call her both "my sister" and "my bride." She is his "sister" as one who shares a common family bond with him in Issachar. And she is his "bride" as the one who has so pledged herself to him—to be his forever, only his. That he only addresses her six times as his "bride" indicates that she is incomplete in that role. She is but "*betrothed* to one husband" (2 Cor. 11:2). Her consummation still looms on the horizon.

Interestingly, the Hebrew word the shepherd uses for his "bride" is *callah*, from *cahlal*, which means "finished, perfected": such is the goal of her calling. How this parallels our own relationship with Jesus! Corporately we are His "sister," for He is our near-Kinsman. And we also are His "bride": as yet incomplete but destined for perfection, for the consummation of our union with Him at His appearing. Almost as if prophetically, the shepherd addresses the Shulammite as one "without blemish, with no flaw, with no spot" (4:7). Paul looks back to this scripture as he envisions the consummation of the marriage of the church to Jesus—"that He might present to Himself the glorious church, having no spot or wrinkle or any such thing; but that she should be holy and blameless" (Eph. 5:27 mg.). In preparation for that day, He calls us away from all that Solomon is—from Lebanon, from Amana, from Senir, from Hermon, from the lions' dens, from the leopards' mountains, from everything that speaks of sin and self and sensuality—that we might simply be His! His forever, only His!

His Ravished Heart

Doubly blessed is every human love which knows the refreshing ongoing expressions of tender joy that appear here: "You have ravished my heart, my sister, my bride...with but one single glance of your eyes" (4:9). It is possible to lose this "first love" in our covenant relationships. The fire could die down, the fervor subside, the enthusiastic expressions dim. But with the ongoing grace of God's presence, we can keep the fires of love fueled and the thoughts of love ever refurbished.

It is staggering to think that Jesus' delight in us could be reflected in the above same words: "You have ravished my heart, my sister, my bride...with but one single glance of your eyes." To think that we, as His bride, so affect the Son of Man! Somehow, in all this, we are beginning to know something of "the riches of the glory of *His* inheritance in the saints" (Eph. 1:18)! How He delights in His bride's glories, in her love, in her very fragrances, in her speech!

His Forever, Only His

The Shulammite's heart had been locked shut to Solomon. "A garden *locked* is my sister, my bride...a spring locked, a fountain sealed up" (4:12). She is available—in all of her inward graces and character—to her beloved *alone.*

Jesus thinks about us in these very same terms. He has called us to Himself *alone*. We are to give nothing of ourselves, ever, to build in Solomon's vain courts. God's Spirit has enriched us with all kinds of choice fruits and spices (see Gal. 5:22-23). We are a veritable "fountain of gardens," for in us is a revival-spring, a "well of living water" (John 4:14); and out of us flow living streams of refreshing (see John 7:38). But this is all *from Him* and *for Him* alone. Ongoing dealings from the Lord alone produce continual fruit, so that the bride cries out: "Awaken, O North Wind—wind of adversity, wind of deeper inward dealings; and come, Wind of the South—comforting wind of God with warm, encouraging breezes! Come, blow upon my garden that its spices may flow out" for my Beloved (4:16)!

When we come into His garden, that is, into enjoyment of our rich inheritance in His church, Jesus will always throw open the doors to a needy and lost world—in order that His bride might become a channel of grace to all men everywhere.

Every true move of God that is wholly given over to Jesus and to the purity of His heavenly vision *does* affect men and women to the very ends of the earth! Thus we understand the mysteries of how a sealed fountain for Jesus alone becomes a *channel* of life to all men everywhere!

For instance, in the history of the Welsh Revival of 1904, Evan Roberts and his "Revival Party" of young people are vivid examples of that passionate and fervent love for Jesus, which, when poured out, became a life-giving river that covered the whole world. Historians have concluded that the Welsh Revival "was the farthest-reaching of all movements…for it affected the whole evangelical cause…." Indeed, the impact of the Welsh Revival was the the foundation of every major outpouring of the Spirit for a century to follow. Thus we can see:

Make me a captive, Lord,
And then I shall be free;
Force me to render up my sword,
And I shall conq'ror be.
I sink in life's alarms
When by myself I stand;
Imprison me within Thine arms,
And strong shall be my hand.

My heart is weak and poor
Until it master find;
It has no spring of action sure,
It varies with the wind.
It cannot freely move
Till Thou hast wrought its chain;
enslave it with Thy matchless love,
And deathless it shall reign.

My will is not my own
Till Thou hast made it Thine;
If it would reach the monarch's throne
It must its crown resign:

It only stands unbent
mid the clashing strife,
When on Thy bosom it has leant,
And found in Thee its life.
—George Matheson (1842–1906)

Heart Searchings Before God

Is my life still blessed with that delight of being "in love"? Am I still living in the joy of a "ravished heart"?

Lord Jesus, my heart is yours alone, my eye is single towards Your heavenly vision. Keep me, by Your Holy Spirit, virgin before You in love, I ask! And from that place of holy consecration, let your rivers of living water pour out from my life upon a dry and barren world! Amen!

Day Ten

ACT FOUR: *Love's Final Choice*

SCENE 1: The Silent Coming of the Shepherd (5:2-8)

The Inspired Story

This act opens in the city of Jerusalem, at the palace of Solomon. This may be the Shulammite's second dream or it may have been an actual happening. She relates (5:2a):

"I was sleeping, but my heart was awake.
A sound! My beloved was knocking!"

These were his words to her (5:26):

"Open to me, my sister, my darling,
My dove, my perfect one!
For my head is filled with dew,
My locks with the drops of the night (from his night travels)."

Motivated again by fear, she tenders a feeble excuse for her procrastination (5:3):

"I have taken off my robe,
How can I put it on?
I have washed my feet, How can I soil them?"

Though outwardly plagued by fear and hesitancies, inwardly her feelings are actually quite different (5:4-6a):

"My beloved extended his hand through the opening,
And my heart yearned for him.
(Then) I rose to open to my beloved;

And my hands dripped with myrrh,
And my fingers with flowing myrrh,
On the handles of the bolt (*he had gone, but he had left behind his scent on the door bolt*).
I opened to my beloved,
But my beloved had withdrawn and was gone!
My soul had gone out (to him) when he spoke!"

She then wraps her veil about her and runs out into the cool, dark night after him; she runs down to the city walls, searching for him (5:6b-7):

"I looked for him, but I did not find him;
I called him but he did not answer me.
The watchmen who made the rounds in the cityfound me,
They struck me and wounded me (*thinking I was up to no good*) until
The watchmen of the walls lifted my veil from me."

Dejectedly returning to the palace, she addresses the court ladies (5:8):

"I charge you, O daughters of Jerusalem,[43]
If you find my beloved,
That you tell him
That I am lovesick—sick, faint with love!"

Devotional Thoughts

We are again in Jerusalem, at the palace, in the harem. It is nighttime, and in her sleep the Shulammite dreams that her beloved shepherd has come to her—in her fears, however, she dreams that she has again turned him away. She rises to pursue him in the streets of Jerusalem, but he has disappeared.

The Pain of Separation

John Deane, in his devotional guide to this Song, describes the pain of separation which springs up between earthly lovers:

> Often love that begins ardent, cools and fades...The cares of life, instead of cementing together, separate. Lack of watchfulness permits grit to enter the bearings and stop the smooth running of hearts' relationships. A hasty word, a bitter spirit, a jealous heart, an ungenerous judgment, a stubborn unbending will, and distance creeps in and widens the gap until little love is left. There [is a]...love-sickness...in which the heart awakes to loss and the absence of the loved one.[44]

A God Who Hides Himself

Perhaps it was fear, uncertainty, or even a cooling of love that caused the Shulammite's initial hesitancy and then the separation between her heart and the heart of her shepherd. It is good for us that our own Shepherd-Lover does not likewise indulge our laziness and our lukewarmness of heart. He has won for Himself this awesome reputation: "Truly, You are a God who hides Himself, O God of Israel, Savior" (Isa. 45:15)! For our own good He will at times withdraw His manifest presence and even hide Himself from us. He wants us to seek Him more fully and search for Him more wholeheartedly: "you will seek Me and find Me, *when* you search for Me with all your heart. 'And I will be found by you,' declares the Lord" (Jer. 29:13-14a). Do you sense a waning of His presence in your life? Do not be dismayed by that discipline; it is but a token of His loving care. He is only seeking to draw you out in a fuller measure in your pursuit of Him. As with any lover, He loves to be pursued; and to those who pursue Him He will manifest Himself!

Our God calls us to that deep exercise of soul called by the mystics, "the pursuit of God": "I rose…I opened…I looked…I called…" Pursue Him, then, and do it with all of your being; yet above all else, pursue Him in *faith*, rising above your feelings; for "without *faith* it is impossible to please Him, for he who comes to God must believe that He is, and that *He is a rewarder of those who seek Him diligently*" (Heb. 11:6). Well may we thank God that these inspired words do not read, "for without *feelings* it is impossible to please Him, for he who comes to God must *feel* that He is…" Faith is the constant exercise of *my spirit* in which I simply choose to take God at His word. The feelings of *my soul* about God may ebb and flow; in the meanwhile, however, God calls me to serve Him "*in my spirit*" (Rom. 1:9)! The hymnwriter describes this whole issue of recapturing God's revival-presence in these words:

Where is the blessedness I knew
When first I saw the Lord?
Where is the soul-refreshing view
Of Jesus and His word?

What peaceful hours I once enjoyed!
How sweet their memory still!
But they have left an aching void
The world can never fill.

Return, O holy Dove, return,
Sweet messenger of rest!
I hate the sins that made Thee mourn
And drove Thee from my breast.

The dearest idol I have known,
Whate'er that idol be,

Help me to tear it from Thy throne,
And worship only Thee.

So shall my walk be close with God,
Calm and serene my frame;
So purer light shall mark the road
That leads me to the Lamb.
—William Cowper (1731–1800)

Heart Searchings Before God

Is there a chilling separation between my soul and my Beloved? Let me deal boldly with those things which have forged the bars of that separation! In my walk with God, is He hiding Himself this day? I will rise up and pursue Him in faith, believing "that He is, and that He is a rewarder of those who seek Him diligently!"

Lord Jesus Christ, my Heavenly Lover, You have bidden me to seek Your face. And Your face I do seek with my whole heart!

Day Eleven

SCENE 2: The Stunning Acclaim of the Shulammite (5:9–6:3)

The Inspired Story

Tthe shepherdess had returned to the palace harem dejected in heart, having failed to find her beloved in the streets of Jerusalem. Now, in answer to her fervent plea to them ("if you find my beloved"—5:8) the women of Solomon's court are stirred to inquire (5:9):

"What is your beloved more than another beloved,
O most beautiful among women?
What is your beloved more than another beloved,
That you charge us so?"[45]

The Shulammite responds in stunning acclamation (5:10-16):
"My beloved is dazzling (bright, radiant) and ruddy,
Marked—lifted up as a banner—among ten thousand.
His head is pure gold, fine gold,
His flowing locks (like palm sprouts) are black as a raven.
His eyes are like doves by the springs of water,
Washed with milk,
Reposed in a setting of fullness.
His cheeks are like a bed of balsam spice,
High banks of aromatic herbs;
His lips are lilies,
Dripping flowing myrrh.
His hands are rods (rings) of gold set with beryl;

His body is carved ivory
Overlaid with (*veins of*) sapphire.
His legs are pillars of marble
Set on bases of fine gold;
His appearance is as Lebanon,
Excellent as the cedars.
His mouth is most sweet.
And all of him is desirable (he is altogether lovely).
This is my beloved and this is my friend,
O daughters of Jerusalem."

At such a description the women of the court can only enthusiastically reply (6:1):

"Where has your beloved gone,
O most beautiful among women?
Where has your beloved faced (turned),
For we seek him with you!"

As best she knows concerning his whereabouts, she answers (6:2-3):

"My beloved went down to his garden,
To the beds of balsam spice
To feed (his flock) in the gardens
And to gather lilies.
I am my beloved's and my beloved is mine,
He feeds (his flock) among the lilies."

Devotional Thoughts

The women of the harem eagerly ask the Shulammite maiden to describe that beloved shepherd for whom she longs. This she does in the most striking of descriptions. They respond, "We seek him with you!" They also now hunger for his presence.

Samuel Medley (1738-99) writes of Jesus:

O could I speak the matchless worth,
O could I sound the glories forth
Which in my Saviour shine!...
I'd sing the characters He bears,
And all the forms of love He wears,
Exalted on His throne...

When stirred to speak of her beloved, the Shulammite does exactly that. She sings of His glory, of "the characters He bears, and all the forms of love He wears." And what a testimony she gives! She does not describe a sterile formula on how to become a follower of his; she does not even describe his works in the earth; she merely describes *him*. She describes each aspect of him and the whole of him together. He is radiant and dazzling. He is singular among ten thousand. He is totally desirable. Above all else, he is *her* beloved and *her* friend. And she speaks of him not only as the sum of all perfection and beauty, but she delineates the aspects of him that, taken together, make up the whole—his head, his flowing locks, his doves' eyes (singular in vision, faithful in integrity), his face, his lips, his hands, his body, his legs, his appearance, his mouth. He is indescribably delightful! The whole of him is desirable!

John the beloved disciple had that same kind of bridal heart. He characterized himself as that disciple who "reclined on Jesus' breast." Can you just see him there—resting his head close on the bosom of Jesus, listening to the firm beat of His strong heart? Little wonder that John more than any other follower of Christ is able to give us such a clear description of the eternal grace and glory of our Lord Jesus. His writings illuminate such themes as Jesus' true deity and His eternity with the Father. If we were to ask John where he uncovered all that insight, he would answer: "In resting on Jesus' bosom."

John begins his first epistle with these choice words: "What was from the beginning, what we have heard, what we have seen with our eyes, what we beheld and our hands handled, concerning the Word of life—" (1 John 1:1). The statement "our hands handled" literally signifies, "our hands stroked"! In my mind's eye I can see John tracing his fingers over the outline of Jesus' face—touching those eyes that had looked with such compassion upon the peoples, moving his fingers over those lips that had spoken such words of forgiveness and acceptance to fallen women and sinful men, touching those hands that had touched and cleansed the leper's rotting sores, I can picture John beholding those very same precious features bruised and battered as his Beloved One was being impaled on a Roman cross outside Jerusalem's walls. His eyes were in torturous pain, His hair matted with blood and sweat, His cheeks streaked with spit and bloody tears, His strong but tender carpenter's hands pierced through with Roman spikes, His lips uttering that one final agonizing cry, "It is finished!" But then I can also visualize John shortly thereafter beholding Him in His resurrection glory, lovingly touching His face and His hands; holding Him closely in a joyous embrace—for He is alive, alive forevermore! "This is my Beloved; and this is my Friend!"

Perhaps in even a more eternally meaningful way—in the Holy Spirit—we today are able to embrace our Lord Jesus, touch Him, to rest our head upon His bosom and enter more fully into the delight of the Shulammite's description of her beloved. This delight must be the essence of our witness and testimony before men. No three- or four-point outline of Acts 2:38 broke the hearts of three thousand on the day of Pentecost; it was Peter's description of Jesus in His exalted glory and majestic beauty (see Acts 2:32-36). "This is my Beloved; and this is my Friend!" Little wonder that the ladies of the court would respond to the Shulammite's words in this fashion: "Where has your beloved gone…for we seek him with you!" I believe we would see far more fruit in our witnessing if, more than His works and more than a formula, we simply declared Him! He is altogether lovely! He is indescribably delightful! The hymn writer sings:

O could I speak the matchless worth,
O could I sound the glories forth
Which in my Saviour shine!
I'd soar, and touch the heavenly strings,
And vie with Gabriel while he sings
In notes almost divine.

I'd sing the precious blood He spilt,
My ransom from the dreadful guilt
Of sin, and wrath Divine,
I'd sing His glorious righteousness,
In which all-perfect, heavenly dress
My soul shall ever shine.

I'd sing the characters He bears,
And all the forms of love He wears
Exalted on His throne:
In loftiest songs of sweetest praise,
I would to everlasting days
Make all His glories known.

Soon, the delightful day will come
When my dear Lord will bring me home,
And I shall see His face,

Then with my Saviour, Brother, Friend,
A blest eternity I'll spend,
Triumphant in His grace.
—Samuel Medley (1738-99)

Heart Searchings Before God

Do I know the Presence of my Beloved One *Himself* in such an intimate way, or am I taken up merely with *things about Him*? Is my testimony of Him a sterile memorized formula about the mechanics of salvation or is my testimony the overflow of a heart deeply in love with the Son of God?

Lord Jesus! You are the sum of all beauty and loveliness, and You have conquered my heart I am enamored with You! You—and You alone—are the great theme on my lips! Jesus!

Day Twelve

SCENE 3: The Statements of King Solomon's Affections (6:4-13)

The Inspired Story

The scene has changed. We now observe the Shulammite alone in Solomon's presence. As he is yet seeking to win her heart to himself, we hear him lavishing his praises on her (6:4):

"You are beautiful, O my darling, as Tirzah (*chief city of northern Israel*),
Lovely as Jerusalem,
Awesome as bannered armies."

She turns to look Solomon fully in the eyes; but unable to bear the purity of her gaze, he cries out in discomfort (6:5a):

"Turn away your eyes from me,
For they confuse (disturb) me...."

It is evident from this last statement that Solomon is not the beloved of the Shulammite, but rather a confused intruder into her life Yet he continues to admire her appealing features (6:5b-7):

"Your hair is like a flock of goats
That have descended (shone) from Gilead.
Your teeth are like a flock of ewes
Which have come up from the washing,
All of which are bearing twins,
And not one among them is barren.
Your temples are like a slice of a pomegranate

From behind your veil."[46]

In Solomon's limited sense of moral values, the Shulammite stands out as the most desirable object in the whole of his harem; nevertheless, there is an awesomeness about her purity (6:8-9a):

"There are sixty queens and eighty concubines,
And maidens without number;
But one is my dove, my perfect one:
She is her mother's one;
She is the choice (pure) one of her who bore her."

Even the other women of the harem recognize that she is remarkably different. Solomon recalls (6:9b-10):

"The daughters saw her and called her blessed,
The queens and the concubines also, and they praised
her (saying):
'Who is this that looks down (grows) like the dawn,
Fair as the (full) moon,
Pure as the sun,
Awesome as bannered armies?'"

The Shulammite then recalls exactly how this whole drama had begun. One day while wandering in the gardens, she suddenly found herself in the midst of Solomon's traveling court (6:11-13):

"I went down to the garden of nut trees
To see the fruits of the valley,
To see whether the vine had blossomed
Or the pomegranates had budded.
Before I was aware, my quest (my looking about) brought me
Among the chariots of the princes of my people—
the King's retinue."
(*I started to flee, but they called after me—*

"Come back, come back, O Shulammite, come back, come back,

that we may gaze upon you!"

(*An onlooker inquires—*)

"Why should you gaze at the Shulammite?"

The retinue replies—

"We would see her in the dance of Mahanaim." (*A local folk dance, called "the sword dance" or "the dance of the two companies."*) *And that is how it all began!*

Devotional Thoughts

Solomon seeks still more fervently to win the Shulammite's heart, but her gaze terrifies him. She is singular, perfect, choice, "fair as the moon, pure as the sun, awesome as bannered armies;" so perfect and so uncompromising. She relates her story of how she ever came to be entangled in this whole affair in the first place—quite innocently, but entangled nonetheless.

John Deane comments on the opening part of this scene:

> Solomon had attempted again and again to win this maiden's heart and now has to confess that she is as terrible as an army with banners…She only frowned on his flatteries and remained unconquerable. In verse 5 he says, 'Turn away those eyes of thine for they have made me afraid.' Her pure eyes with their strong, steady, penetrating gaze were more than he could meet. Purity gives majesty to the soul…Solomon was rebuked by this simple…maid. He was cowed. Her presence with its purity and strength made him afraid. His inner life told him that she was right and he was wrong. He could not face her gaze. She was terrible as an army with banners.[47]

Solomon's words in 6:5-7 are identical to those in 4:1-3. Deane comments on this point in this way: "Mark the extravagance of the king's flattery and its total lack of originality. He could only repeat his former phrases about the physical beauty of the girl."[48] The insincerity of this entire scene is even further reflected by his total insensitivity in comparing her with his surrounding "sixty queens and eighty concubines, and maidens without number" (6:8). In days gone by Solomon had painstakingly wooed them all and had won them; but now a new cluster of dates has ripened and he is reaching out to pluck it (a figure of speech Solomon himself uses as recorded in 7:7-8).

In the midst of his insensitive comparisons, however, Solomon is awed by the Shulammite's uniqueness, perfection and purity (6:9). Even the ladies of the court are stunned by her awesome purity. She stands "*fair* as the (full) moon, *pure* as the sun, *awesome* as an army with banners" (6:10). Her surroundings in the harem have not cheapened her. She has not sold herself for the benefits of the harem's luxury and ease. She is still reserved alone for her tremendous lover.

How clearly this all speaks to us of a pilgrim people in these last days, of a bridal company untainted by the courts of this fallen world system, of a people passionate in the pursuit of their Tremendous Lover. Out of wholesome earthly courtships, strong earthly marriages, and vibrant godly families the Bride of Christ is being formed in these final days!

The Bride in the Midst of the Harem

The Lord Jesus is searching for purity of heart in this generation. In this present evil world, may we stand like the Shulammite—perfect, unique, pure as the sun, terrible as an army with banners! John Wesley (1703-91), a powerful eighteenth century revivalist in England, wrote about such ruthlessness and abandon in the earth:

Is there a thing beneath the sun
That strives with Thee my heart to share?
Ah, tear it thence, and reign alone,
The Lord of every motion there!
Then shall my heart from earth be free,
When it hath found repose in Thee.

Each moment draw from earth away
My heart, that lowly waits Thy call;
Speak to my inmost soul, and say,
"I am thy love, thy God, thy all."
To feel Thy power, to hear Thy voice,
To taste Thy love, be all my choice.

Heart Searchings Before God

Am I pure before my God? Am I faithful and loyal in my marriage, in my family, in my walk with Jesus? Do I stand in the midst of Solomon's harem as one uncompromisingly "pure as the sun, awesome as an army with banners"?

Lord Jesus, I follow hard after you with holy abandon, with fervent passion, in total commitment to Your heart's purposes for this generation!

Day Thirteen

SCENE 4: The Shulammite's Final Break (7:1–8:4)

The Inspired Story

The scene is now set in Solomon's harem. The ladies of the court are vigorously seeking—in the fleshy, sensual language of the court—to encourage the Shulammite as they dress her (7:1-5):

"How beautiful are your footsteps in sandals,
O daughter of Nadib (O noble daughter).
The curves of your thighs are like jewels,
The work of the hands of an artisan.
Your navel is a round goblet
Which never lacks mixed wine;
Your belly is a heap of wheat
Hedged about with lilies.
Your two breasts are like two fawns,
Twins of a gazelle.
Your neck is a tower of ivory,
Your eyes—(like) the fish pools in Heshbon
By the gate of Bathrabbim;
Your nose is a tower of Lebanon,
Which faces peering toward Damascus.
Your head crowns you (like) Carmel,
And the flowing hair of your head is like purple (threads);
The King is held captive in (your) tresses!"

At this moment Solomon himself steps forward to receive her (7:6-9a):

"How beautiful and how pleasant you are,
My love, in all your delights!
This stature of yours is like a palm tree,
And your breasts are like clusters of grapes.
I said, 'I will climb the palm tree,
I will take hold of its fruit stalks.'
Oh please may your breasts be like clusters of the vine,
And the scent of your breath like apples,
And your mouth like the best wine—"

The Shulammite boldly cuts Solomon off in the middle of his statement and exclaims (7:9b):
"—It goes down smoothly (uprightly) for my beloved,
Flowing gently through the lips of those who fall asleep."

She then boldly tells Solomon of her firm commitment to her dear shepherd-lover (7:10):
"I am my beloved's,
And his desire is towards me—we are committed to each other!"

She then cries out for her beloved to come and take her away from Solomon's courts (7:11–8:2):
"Come, my beloved, let us go forth to the field,
Let us lodge (spend the night) in the villages.
Let us go early to the vineyards;
Let us see whether the vine has flowered
And its blossoms have opened,
And whether the pomegranates have brought forth buds.
There I will give you my loves (my caresses).
The love apples (mandrakes) have given forth fragrance;

And over our doors are all excellent fruits,
Both new and old,
Which I have laid up for you, my beloved.
Oh that you were like a brother to me
Who nursed at my mother's breasts?
(Then) if I found you outside. I would kiss you, (and)
No one would despise me, either (for in Mid-Eastern culture, to kiss a brother publicly would be acceptable).
I would lead you, I would bring you
Into my mother's house; you would instruct me:
I would make you drink spiced wine from the juice of my pomegranates."

And in a final cry of desperation she pleads (8:3):
"Let his left hand be under my head,
And his right hand embrace me."

Solomon, realizing again the apparent hopelessness of winning the Shulammite's heart, addresses the women of the court for the last time (8:4):
"I charge you, O daughters of Jerusalem,
Why should you stir up or why should you awaken my love,
Until she pleases?"—*an hour he shall never see!*

Devotional Thoughts

The women of Solomon's harem seek to stir the heart of the Shulammite to consider her own astounding beauty and her own desirability in Solomon's eyes. Solomon himself appears, seeking to woo the shepherdess; but in the very midst of his bold advances the Shulammite cuts him off, for she is committed to another—her beloved shepherd—with all her heart. She desires him to come and take her to the fields and to the villages of their native Issachar. She is his and his alone.

In words that are almost an embarrassment to the sensitive reader, the ladies of Solomon's court describe the Shulammite, from head to toe, as they dress her for Solomon's appearance (7:1-5). The tenor of their statements is so very different from the shepherd's gracious description of the Shulammite in 4:7-15; they clearly speak from a sensual mind-set.

At a certain point in these proceedings Solomon himself steps forward to receive the Shulammite. He compliments her intimate bodily parts, stating his desire to intrude into her virgin purity, to climb her tree and take hold of her fruit stalks (7:7-8). She suddenly cuts him off and declares in the boldest of terms the mutual commitment between the shepherd and herself: "I am my beloved's and his desire is towards me!" (7:10) She expresses longing for her lover to come and lead her from Solomon's palaces into the fields and the villages and the vineyards in which she is so very much at home. She has even stored up for her handsome shepherd all kinds of modest but loving gifts—strings of both new and old fruits, fresh and dried. She longs for his embraces (8:3). Finally, in the face of her clear and absolute commitment, Solomon and his court can only back away from trying to entice her any more to run after the king! (8:4)

In this act we have surely touched the very core message of this book—pure and undefiled bridal love, wholly faithful and totally loyal. It is a true example to every believing heart. Let us take a deep look into the eyes of this humble but beautiful shepherdess from Issachar and into the eyes of her beloved shepherd. Witness how she defies all of Solomon's allurements and holds firmly to her shepherd's love. Witness, too, how patiently he, in turn, waits for her commitment, undergirding her with his love and with his utter faithfulness. Let us now offer up in the presence of God our own friendships, engagements, marriages, and families—bathing them all in the holy light of this beautiful commitment between the lovers from Shunem. Let us preeminently hold up before God our love relationship with our Lord Jesus Christ, radiant in the light of the glory of this beauty and grace that we have witnessed. Of our relationship with Him, our conclusions must truly be:

Jesus, priceless treasure,
Source of purest pleasure,
Truest friend to me;
Long my heart hath panted,
Till it well-nigh fainted,
Thirsting, Lord, for Thee.
Thine I am, O spotless Lamb,
I will suffer nought to hide Thee
Ask for nought beside Thee.

Fare thee well that errest,
Thou that earth preferrest,
Thou wilt tempt in vain;
Fare thee well, transgression,
Hence, abhorred possession,
Come not forth again...
Yea, whate'er I here must bear,
Thou art still my purest pleasure,
Jesus, priceless treasure.
—Johann Franck (1618-77)

Heart Searchings Before God

Am I full of those little things which please my Beloved, my heavenly Lover?

Lord Jesus Christ, You are my purest pleasure, my priceless treasure! Make me, by the power of Your Holy Spirit, Your true and loyal lover! Amen!

ACT FIVE: *Love's Endless Triumph*

SCENE 1: THE SHEPHERD AND THE SHULAMMITE JOINED FOREVER (8:5-14)

The Inspired Story

When the loving shepherd hears of the Shulammite's final decision to break totally with Solomon, he loses no time in coming for her. The final act opens as they are on their journey home together. Seeing them approach, a passerby inquires (8:5a):

"Who is this coming up from the wilderness,
Leaning on her beloved?"

As they view the scene of the Shulammite's childhood, the shepherd recalls (8:5b):

"Beneath the apple tree I awakened you—
There your mother travailed for you; there she travailed[49] that birthed you."

The Shulammite and her handsome lover converse together[50] (8:6):

"Set me as a seal upon your heart,[51]
As a seal upon your arm.
For love is strong as death—*as irreversible and as final*!
Jealousy (passion) is as severe (unyielding) as Sheol (the grave).
Its flames are flames of fire
The very flame of Jehovah."

They continue speaking,[52] *recalling their recent painful experiences involving Solomon* (8:7):

"Many waters cannot quench love,

Nor can floods drown it (sweep it away).

If a man (*such as Solomon*) would give all the wealth of his house for love,

It (he) would be utterly despised—trampled upon."

Some of the maiden's brothers, walking with the shepherd and the Shulammite in the way, ask for advice on another situation (8:8):

"We have a little sister,

And she has no breasts:

What shall we do for our sister

On the day when he speaks for her (when she is spoken for—in marriage)?"

The shepherd and the Shulammite give their counsel (8:9):

"If she is a wall (*a virgin and not accessible*),

We shall build on her a battlement of silver (*we'll protect her*),

but if she is a door (*accessible and promiscuous*),

We shall barricade her with bonds of cedar (*we'll discipline and protect her!*)."

The Shulammite then gives her own triumphant testimony (8:10):

"I have been a wall (*I kept my virgin purity throughout this entire ordeal*),

And my breasts were like (*inaccessible*) towers.

Then—(*as a result*) I became in his (*Solomon's*) eyes as one finding peace—*as one to be respected and granted peace from this ordeal*."

The Shulammite further describes some of the difficulties of having been involved with Solomon (8:11-12):

"Solomon had a vineyard at Baalhamon;

He entrusted the vineyard to caretakers;

Each one was to bring (*to Solomon*) a thousand (*pieces*) of silver for its fruits.

(*But*) I kept my very own vineyard to myself.

The thousand (*pieces of silver*) are for you, Solomon.

And two hundred (*about twenty percent*) are for those who take care of its fruit."

Then losing sight of all of these past distracting happenings, the bridegroom turns his eyes on his bride (8:13):

"O you who sit in the gardens,

My companions are listening for your voice (*in song*)—Let me hear it!"

She can only answer him with fullest expectation and anticipation (8:14):

"Hurry—make haste—my beloved,

And be like a gazelle or a young stag

(*and take me to our waiting homes*[53])

On the mountains of spices!"

"…**and so shall we ever be with the Lord**" (1 Thess. 4:17b). Amen!

Devotional Thoughts

The shepherd comes to take the Shulammite home with him from Solomon's courts. Coming up from the wilderness they arrive in Issachar, the Shulammite leaning on her beloved shepherd's arm. As they walk together, they pass familiar childhood scenes while discussing their past painful experiences involving Solomon.

The little poetic drama closes with the shepherd's sole desire to hear the Shulammite's voice in the gardens and her sole desire to be with him forever!

John Deane introduces this final act with these observations:

Solomon realized that it was useless to pursue his wooing of one so faithful and loyal, so pure and strong: and he set her free to return to her village home…The first lines of 8:5 contain the question of the villagers as they see the two lovers coming back home, hand in hand, and plainly the lassie is now leaning heavily on her beloved. Then he speaks in 8:5, the latter half of the verse, reminding her of a sacred spot where her heart awoke to his love…Has not love its memories of secluded spots? Beside the rippling waters or where shafts of light make of tall trees cathedral columns and high windows?…Life is not just acts and words and things. It is relationships; it is love and trust and worship…

No floods can ever quench this love; no rivers drown it. If a man offers all that he has for love he would be utterly despised [see 8:7]. This is the centre and the secret and the climax of the scene. For this the Song was written. This is God's picture of true love. This is His love. It is the love for which He has made us capable. It is the ideal He had in mind when He made man and brought to him the partner He had planned and formed for him…Oh, that Christian hearts sought more of the tender human love of this Book….

> True love is a flame of Jehovah (see 8:6], a spark of supernatural fire kindled and cherished by God...How mighty and resistless is the love of our Lover God, and how rightly jealous He is of our love....
>
> Solomon sought to buy this lady's love. He took her to his court and showed her its luxury and wealth. He took her to his country home and paraded there his pomp. He tried flattering blandishments and sensuous appeal. But nothing can buy love. ["If a man offered all he has for love, he would be utterly despised" (8:7)]....
>
> Have you turned aside from your first love? "Return, return O Shulammite, to thy Tremendous Lover."[54]

It is precious that this entire drama ends on two most beautiful notes. As all the past distracting events fade into the background, the shepherd-bridegroom has but one great desire: "Let me hear your voice." Jesus has one great delight too: to hear the voice of His beloved Bride in praise, prayer, and adoration. And her one great desire? "Take me to our waiting home on the mountains of spices!" She longs only to be forever with him! She cherished his presence. Paul summed it up in his Thessalonian statement, "And so shall we *ever* be *with* the Lord" (4:17b). What a joy! What a delight! Hallelujah! O, come, Lord Jesus; come! Hurry—make haste—O our Beloved! We welcome Your glad returning!

"And so shall we ever be with You, Lord!"

Separated unto Jesus,
Loos'd from all the world beside,
Blinded by the Advent glory,
Hour by hour would I abide.

He is coming! He is coming!
Pass the heavenly watchword on.
Go ye forth to meet the Bridegroom,
Hail! to God's anointed Son.

See the Advent glory breaking!
Faith will soon be lost in sight,
Face to face I shall behold Him,
Bathed in His eternal light!

—E. May Grimes

Heart Searchings Before God

"So shall we ever be with the Lord." Is such a thought my greatest anticipation in life? Is my greatest eagerness to see the face of Jesus, to be with Him forever? Lord Jesus, You are my "Tremendous Lover"!

"Come, Lord Jesus!" (Rev. 22.20b) *O, Come!*

Amen!

Endnotes

1. A possible alternate reading is: "The Song of Songs, about (of, or, concerning) Solomon"—which could make the author another besides Solomon, writing about Solomon.
2. 1 Kings 4:32
3. 1:1,5; 3:7,9,11; 8:11-12
4. 1 Samuel 23:16-29
5. Revelation 2:4
6. Ephesians 1:6
7. Ephesians 5:27, from Song 4:7
8. Song 6:8
9. 1 Kings 11:1-2b
10. 1 Kings 11:3a
11. 1 Kings 11:2c
12. 1 Kings 11:1-7
13. John A. Balchin, "The Song of Solomon," in D. Guthrie and J. A. Motyers, eds., *The New Bible Commentary: Revised*, 3rd ed. (Grand Rapids, Mich.: William B. Eerdmans Publishing Company, 1970), 579. (Copyright 1970 by Inter-Varsity Press, London). This commentary takes the point of view we ourselves take in this present commentary on the Song.
14. Matthew 12:39-41
15. Matthew 12:42
16. 1 Kings 7:2, Amplified
17. Joshua 19:17-18
18. An important verse in this interpretation.

19. Song 6:13, where Shulammite is a by-form of Shunammite (this latter being a feminine adjective derived from Shunem). Shulammite is feminine for "Solomon." Though Solomon sought to alter her name to be like his, he could not alter her heart to be like his!

20. In providing within the Inspired Story segment a translation for the Song of Songs, I have used the New American Standard Bible as my basic tool (although not observing its employment of italics in every case). I have changed the wording used, however, when, in the various other versions consulted, the translators, by consensus, had supplied a clearer, more accurate English word (or words) for the original Hebrew. Moreover, in between the various verses, I have inserted italic notations as to the *probable* speakers (realizing that the original notations of Solomon as to who is speaking are now lost to us). Also in italics have been added as well something of the possible backdrop for each of the many scenes.

Thus, all words in the Inspired Story segment that appear in italics, including the insertions in parentheses in the Scripture text, are not part of the Hebrew text but are added to bring out more clearly the sense of the text. Finally, the reader should note that insertions in parentheses which appear in regular type are a part of the expanded meaning of the Hebrew text.

21. As quoted in John Deane, *This Tremendous Lover: Meditations on the Song of Solomon* (Auckland, New Zealand.: The Institute Printing and Publishing Society Ltd., 1953), 18.

22. As quoted in Ibid., 18.

23. Amy Carmichael, as quoted by Edwin J. Orr, *Evangelical Awakenings in South Asia* (Minneapolis, Minn: Bethany, 1975), 133.

24. Amplified Bible.

25. John Deane, op. cit., 18-19.

26. *The Amplified Old Testament, Part Two (Job-Malachi)* (Grand Rapids, Mich.: Zondervan Publishing House, 1962), 449.

27. Amplified Bible.

28. Love: feminine; hence, a reference to the Shulammite.

29. William E. Allen, *History of Revivals and Worldwide Revival Movements* (Antrim, N. Ireland: Revival Publishing Col, 1951), 35.

30. "The winter" refers to the rainy season, at the end of which the growing season starts (in March and April).

31. In the Middle East, doves nest in the cliffs (see Jer. 48:28).

32. In our story it is obvious that the Shulammite herself was both a vinedresser (1:6; 7:12; 8:12) and a shepherdess (1:8). And her shepherd-lover was also a vinedresser (2:15), as well as a sheepherder (1:7; 2:16; 6:2-3). King Solomon, in all his royal majesty and wealth, had indeed both herds and vineyards (8:11); but *he himself was not a sheeptender and a vinedresser by vocation*. By this it is quite clear that King Solomon and the unobtrusive shepherd are two different persons in the story, and that this unobtrusive one becomes to us the true picture of our lowly Shepherd-Lover in all of His beauty and simplicity.

33. Separation: *bether* in Hebrew, meaning "cleavage"—from the root "to cut in two;" thus, she bids him depart.

34. John Deane, *op. cit.*, 25.

35. The Hebrew word for "night" is plural thus indicating that it was "night after night" in which she dreamed of searching for him.

36. Amplified Bible, Song 2:7.

37. Love: feminine; again, the maiden is in view.

38. A.W. Tozer, *The Pursuit of God* (Harrisburg, Pa.: Christian Publications, Inc., 1948), 15.

39. This may well be a reference to what was probably Solomon's original marriage—to the daughter of the Pharaoh of Egypt (1 Kings 3:1). This in itself was disobedience in Solomon's life: to mingle the seed of Israel with the seed of pagan Egypt. Consequently, Solomon built for her a separate house, lest she would come near to defile the place where the glorious presence of the Ark of Jehovah had been in the house of David (1 Kings 7:8; 2 Chron. 8:11). To this disobedience was then added multiplied sins, for "King Solomon loved many foreign women along with the daughter of Pharaoh" until ultimately "he had seven hundred wives" (1 Kings 11:1,3). In the theme of this Song, which is pure bridal love, Solomon represents for us no true type of Christ Jesus our Lord. He regrettably stands rather as a type of fallenness and spiritual adultery, the spirit of antichrist.

40. It is of interest to note that only in Solomon's presence is the Shulammite veiled (4:1,3; 6:7). In the presence of her shepherd she is uncovered and disclosed (1:7).

41. "Notice the complete change of character in this address of the beloved shepherd from that of the previous ones of the sensuous king."—*The Amplified Old Testament, Part Two (Job-Malachi)*, 455 footnote. Another has observed similarly at this very same juncture: "How chaste and pure and pulsating it [the shepherd's address in song 4:1-15] is beside the coarse and sensuous expressions of his rival king" found in 4:1-5.—John Deane, *op. cit.*, 37. It is Song 4:7 that Paul applies in Ephesians 5:27 to the church: a Bride without spot, without flaw, without blemish.

42. Amana, Senir and Hermon are all in the Lebanon area.

43. Rather than closing Act Three after 5:1, Solomon as author may have actually closed Act Three at this juncture (5:8). This is because of the presence of that familiar refrain which also concludes the other acts, "I charge you, O daughters of Jerusalem…" (2:7, 3:5, 8:4).

44. John Deane, *op. cit.*, 41.

45. It is evident from this inquiry that Solomon is not in view, for there would be no need to ask such a question were he indeed the beloved for whom she longs. The ladies of the court were all too wellacquainted with Solomon.

46. Notice the identicalness of these words to Solomon's earlier praises in 4:2-3. These are probably the words which Solomon spoke, by rote, to the many in the harem that he is about to allude to.

47. John Deane, *op. cit.*, 40-50.

48. John Deane, *op. cit.*, 50.

49. An alternate reading for *travailed* is *pledged*—"she pledged you."

50. This, especially, is a portion of the Song in which it is difficult to determine who is saying what to whom. Yet perhaps it is not unlike what we find in the Book of Revelation where both the Lord (1:15) and His Bride (19:6) are so united in heart that they have come to sound very much alike—"like the sound of many waters."

51. In olden days, a seal with which a man made his signature was carried by him suspended from his neck over his heart (cf. Gen. 38:18).

52. Again, it is unclear who is saying what to whom. See footnote on 8:6.

53. Amplified Bible.

54. John Deanc, *op. cit.*, 57, 59.

Other Books by
Charles and Dotty Schmitt

Floods Upon the Dry Ground
A History of the Church by Charles Schmitt

The history of the Christian faith is the most important and most inspiring study that one can undertake next to the study of the Holy Scriptures themselves. As with Alex Haley in his novel Roots, there is something within Christians wanting to know the simple facts of their origins. Hence this book. Here is the story of your roots!

(Second edition; 169 pages)

The Delight of Being His Daughter
by Dotty Schmitt

Dotty Schmitt honestly shares principles of marriage that go beyond a mere surface look at the subject. As she learned the true meaning of love for her husband, God honored her obedience and helped her and her husband grow spiritually. Dotty Schmitt's positive view of life, love and marriage will introduce you to a new way of living.

(Fourth edition; 152 pages)

The Bride Wears Combat Boots
by Dotty Schmitt

This is Dotty's second ful-length book, melding together two great themes—the bridal call of the Church to a deep, intimate walk with God and the call of the Church to spiritual warfare as the veritable army of God. A book you will want to read!

To Soar Again
by Charles Schmitt

Charles traces the dealings of God in his own personal life over the past twelve years. This is the account of one man's journey from woundedness to wholeness, written as an encouragement to all who have been "wounded sore by the archer's arrow." Charles discusses in-depth the divine process of healing, the renewing of spiritual strength and the mounting up on eagle's wings to soar again in the purposes of God!

Foundational Teachings

A periodical containing articles of current spiritual concern written by Charles and Dotty Schmitt and other authors. This periodical is presently being sent to all 50 United States and to over 80 nations, declaring the wonders of Christ and His Church. You will want to order your free subscription today!

For additional information, write:

Foundational Teachings of Immanuel's Church
16819 New Hampshire Ave.
Silver Spring, MD 20905, USA
or call (301) 989-HOPE (4673)
or FAX (301) 989-1640
www.immanuels.org